WOULD you RATHER...

WOULD you RATHER...

#1

Have a magical Christmas tree that grows presents for all your friends

OR

Have a magical holiday mailbox that sends heartfelt letters to your loved ones

#2

Have a snowball fight with talking snowflakes

OR

Build a snow castle with singing icicles

#3

Have a Christmas dinner with historical figures from the past

OR

Have a Christmas dinner with characters from your favorite animated movies

#4

Spend Christmas on an adventure with pirates

OR

Spend Christmas in a land filled with talking animals

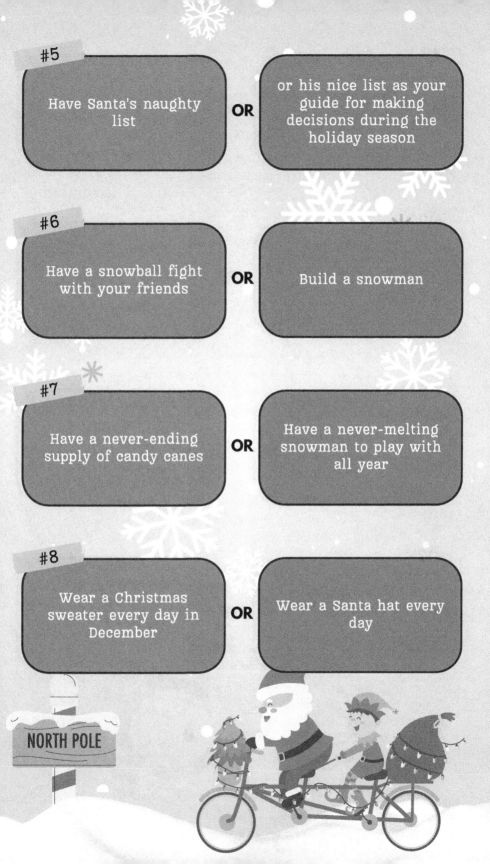

#5

Have Santa's naughty list

OR

or his nice list as your guide for making decisions during the holiday season

#6

Have a snowball fight with your friends

OR

Build a snowman

#7

Have a never-ending supply of candy canes

OR

Have a never-melting snowman to play with all year

#8

Wear a Christmas sweater every day in December

OR

Wear a Santa hat every day

NORTH POLE

#9

Receive presents every hour for one day

OR

Receive one big present at the end of the holiday season

#10

Visit a Christmas carnival with rides and games

OR

Visit a winter festival with ice sculptures and light displays

#11

Have a Christmas filled with friendly talking animals

OR

Have a Christmas where everything is made of candy and treats

#12

Spend Christmas on a tropical island with talking dolphins

OR

Spend Christmas in a winter wonderland with talking snowmen

#13

Have a Christmas in a magical winter wonderland

OR

Have a Christmas on a space station overlooking Earth

#14

Have a Christmas where it's always snowing but never cold

OR

Have a Christmas where it's warm but the snow is made of cotton candy

#15

Spend a day with Santa's reindeer, learning their favorite holiday games

OR

Spend a day with a group of friendly yetis, solving riddles in a snowy cave

#16

Help Santa decorate his sleigh with colorful lights

OR

Design a new outfit for Rudolph the Red-Nosed Reindeer

#17

Have a Christmas party with all your favorite fictional characters

OR

Have a Christmas party with all your real friends and family

#18

Have a pet reindeer that can talk and tell jokes

OR

Have a pet snowman that can play hide-and-seek with you

#19

Decorate a gingerbread house

OR

Make Christmas ornaments

#20

Have a Christmas tree that changes ornaments every day

OR

Have a tree that sparkles with different colors every minute

NORTH POLE

#21

Be Santa's chief gift wrapper

OR

Be the head of the North Pole's hot cocoa department

#22

Have a talking pet snowman

OR

Have a pet reindeer that can sing your favorite songs

#23

Have a Christmas morning full of surprises

OR

Have a Christmas evening with lots of laughter and games

#24

Go caroling with your friends

OR

Read a Christmas story by the fireplace

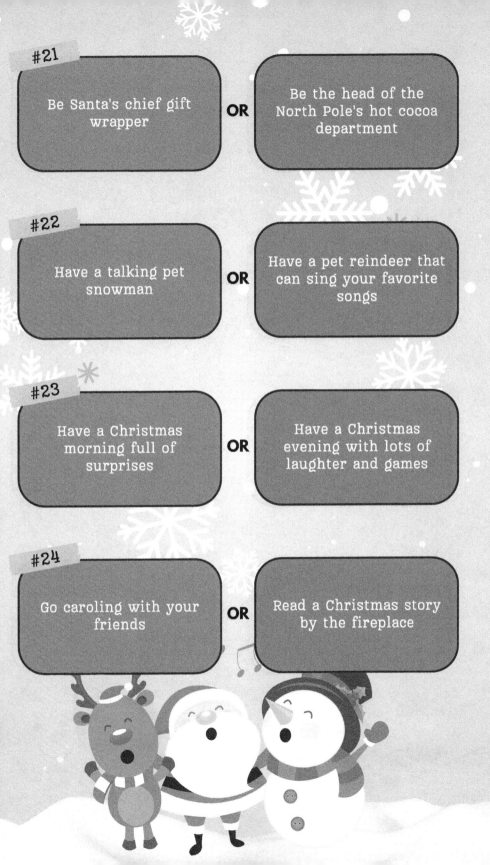

#25

Visit a Christmas carnival with games and rides

OR

Explore a winter wonderland with hidden treasures to discover

#26

Have a Christmas filled with surprises from secret admirers

OR

Have a day where you can grant wishes to others

#27

Make it snow every time you sneeze

OR

Jingle whenever you laugh

#28

Have a magical scarf that keeps you warm no matter how cold it gets

OR

Have a bell that only rings when Santa is nearby

#29

Spend Christmas with superheroes who protect the holiday spirit

OR

Spend Christmas with fairies who can make your holiday dreams come true

#30

Help the Grinch find the true meaning of Christmas

OR

Teach Frosty the Snowman to dance

#31

Have a giant gingerbread house as your home

OR

Have a candy cane forest in your backyard

#32

Have a magical sleigh that can take you anywhere in the world

OR

Have a magical snow globe that lets you visit any place in history

NORTH POLE

#33

Spend Christmas in a cozy cabin with a fireplace

OR

Spend Christmas in a magical castle with talking paintings

#34

Have a Christmas with giant, friendly monsters

OR

Have a Christmas with tiny, playful elves as your helpers

#35

Have hot chocolate with marshmallows

OR

Have a bowl of your favorite ice cream for dessert on Christmas

#36

Receive a special gift from a secret admirer every day until Christmas

OR

Have a letter from Santa with clues to find hidden treasures

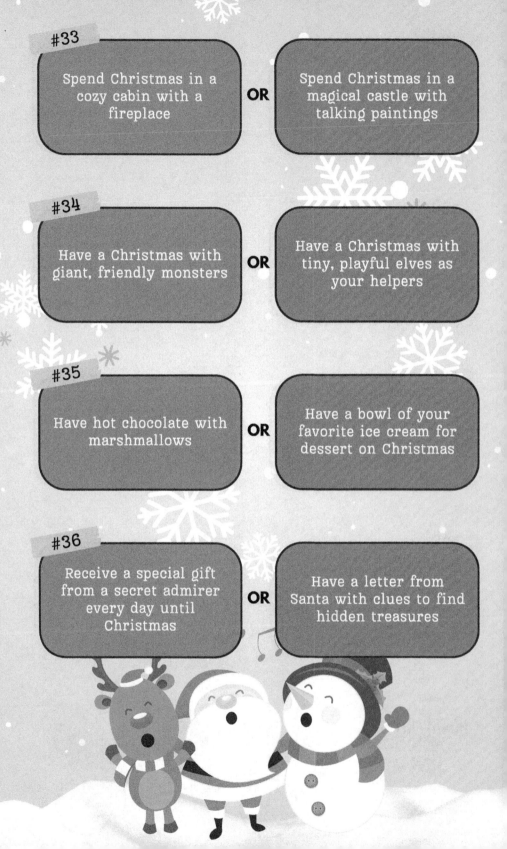

#37

Spend Christmas with your favorite cartoon characters

OR

Spend Christmas with your favorite superheroes

#38

Spend Christmas on a magical flying carpet with talking ornaments

OR

Spend Christmas in a cozy cottage with a fireplace that tells holiday jokes

#39

Have a gingerbread house that can change its shape and size

OR

Have a snow globe that can make it snow inside your room whenever you want

#40

Have a sled that can race on clouds

OR

Have a hat that can change your hair into any holiday color

#41

Help the elves build toys

OR

Be Santa's official taste-tester for cookies and milk

#42

Have a Christmas without any gifts but full of love and laughter

OR

Have a Christmas with lots of gifts but less time with family and friends

#43

Have a Christmas with endless holiday movies but no holiday treats

OR

Have a Christmas with delicious treats but no movies

#44

Have a sled that can go uphill without any effort

OR

Have a pair of boots that let you walk on clouds

NORTH POLE

#45

Have a Christmas tree that sparkles with colorful lights

OR

Have a Christmas tree that glows with golden lights

#46

Have a magical holiday cape that allows you to fly

OR

Have a pair of magical boots that let you jump as high as the North Pole

#47

Sing your favorite Christmas song in front of your family

OR

Perform a Christmas dance

#48

Have a sled that can go uphill without any effort

OR

Have a magical cape that can make you invisible on Christmas

#49

Have a magical sleigh ride with your favorite Christmas characters

OR

Visit Santa's workshop and make your own toy

#50

Spend Christmas with your favorite mythical creatures

OR

Spend Christmas with characters from classic holiday TV shows

#51

Ride on a sleigh pulled by flying dogs

OR

Ride on a roller coaster made of holiday lights

#52

Be a gingerbread cookie decorating pro

OR

Be a snowflake-catching champion

#53

Have a magical hat that can create your favorite holiday-themed food

OR

Have a pair of boots that allow you to walk on water

#54

Have a Christmas filled with surprises and no planning

OR

Have a Christmas with carefully planned activities and games

#55

Have a talking parrot that repeats your favorite holiday stories

OR

Have a snow globe that can show you scenes from your dream vacation

#56

Have a magical snow globe that lets you visit the past

OR

Have a magical snow globe that shows the future

NORTH POLE

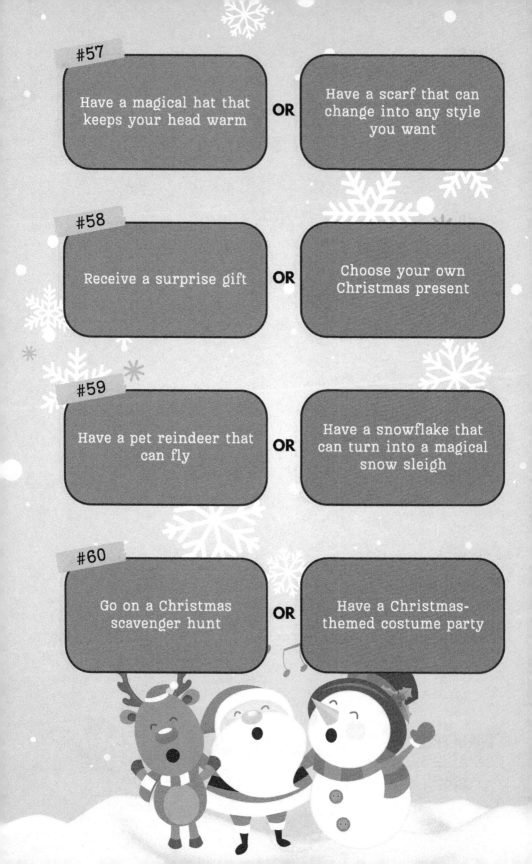

#57

Have a magical hat that keeps your head warm

OR

Have a scarf that can change into any style you want

#58

Receive a surprise gift

OR

Choose your own Christmas present

#59

Have a pet reindeer that can fly

OR

Have a snowflake that can turn into a magical snow sleigh

#60

Go on a Christmas scavenger hunt

OR

Have a Christmas-themed costume party

#61

Leave out milk and cookies for Santa

OR

Leave out carrots for his reindeer

#62

Have a snowball fight with friendly monsters

OR

Decorate a gingerbread village with mischievous elves

#63

Have a magical holiday songbook that plays music by itself

OR

Have a talking ornament that shares fun facts about Christmas

#64

Go ice skating on a frozen pond with talking fish

OR

Have a snowball fight with a group of friendly yetis

#65

Spend Christmas with characters from your favorite video games

OR

Spend Christmas with characters from your favorite fairytale books

#66

Spend Christmas in a cozy cabin in the mountains with a talking fireplace

OR

Spend Christmas in a beach house with a friendly sandcastle that comes to life

#67

Have a candy cane that grows when you water it

OR

Have a gingerbread house that can shrink to fit in your pocket

#68

Have a Christmas tree that glows in the dark

OR

Have a Christmas tree that changes colors every hour

NORTH POLE

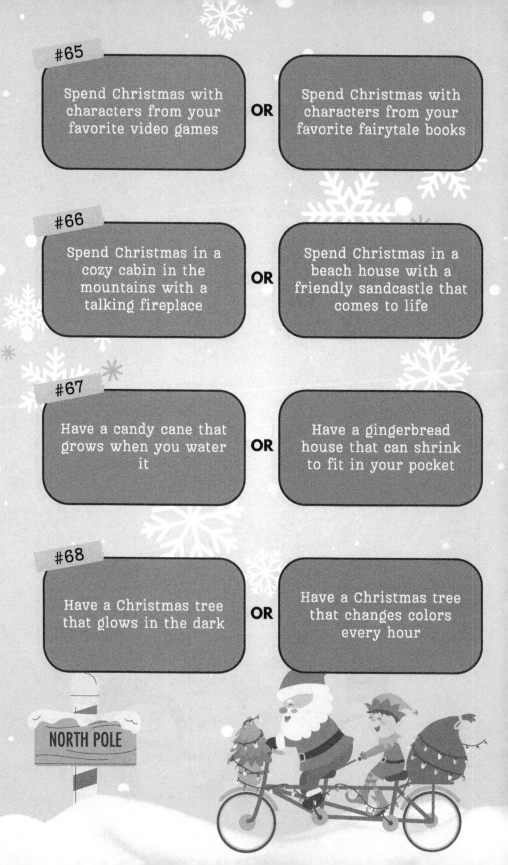

#69

Have a Christmas dinner with all your favorite movie characters

OR

Have a Christmas dinner with all your favorite video game characters

#70

Have the ability to make it snow on Christmas day wherever you go

OR

Have the ability to make it sunny and warm no matter where you are

#71

Have a pet snowman that can perform magic tricks

OR

Have a magical gingerbread house that can bake your favorite treats

#72

Watch a Christmas movie every day until Christmas

OR

Open one present every day until Christmas

#73

Have a treehouse that's a cozy cottage with a roaring fireplace

OR

Have a treehouse that's a pirate ship soaring through the snowy skies

#74

Have a Christmas where it's always nighttime with twinkling stars

OR

Have a Christmas where it's always daytime with snowflakes falling from the sky

#75

Stay up all night to catch a glimpse of Santa

OR

Wake up super early to open presents before anyone else

#76

Only eat candy canes for a day

OR

Drink hot cocoa all day long

#77

Have an indoor snowball fight with your friends

OR

Have a beach party with your family on Christmas day

#78

Have a snowman that tells jokes

OR

Have a talking parrot that sings Christmas carols

#79

Have a holiday-themed snow globe that plays music

OR

Have a Christmas-themed storybook that comes to life

#80

Have a Christmas with endless fireworks in the sky

OR

Have a Christmas with a magical light show

NORTH POLE

#81

Spend Christmas with superheroes who fight for justice

OR

Spend Christmas with fairytale characters from your favorite stories

#82

Have a holiday season where you can talk to animals

OR

Have a season where you can bring inanimate objects to life

#83

Spend Christmas at the North Pole with Santa

OR

Spend Christmas in a magical kingdom with talking animals

#84

Have a snow globe that shows a winter wonderland

OR

Have a snow globe with a miniature Santa's workshop inside

#85

Have a talking Christmas tree

OR

Have a talking snowman as your holiday companion

#86

Have a gingerbread house that can change its flavor to your liking

OR

Have a magical holiday lantern that lights up with your favorite colors

#87

Have a pet reindeer that can tell you jokes

OR

Have a snowman that can transform into any type of vehicle

#88

Get a surprise visit from a holiday hero like Frosty

OR

Get a surprise visit from a friendly alien from another planet who loves Christmas

#89

Make a snow angel in the snow

OR

Build a snow fort

#90

Have a treehouse that's a cozy winter cabin with a fireplace

OR

Have a treehouse that's a pirate ship sailing through the snowy skies

#91

Have a real-life elf as your best friend

OR

Be able to communicate with animals like Dr. Dolittle during Christmas

#92

Spend Christmas at the North Pole with Santa's elves

OR

Spend Christmas in a snowy kingdom with talking snowmen

NORTH POLE

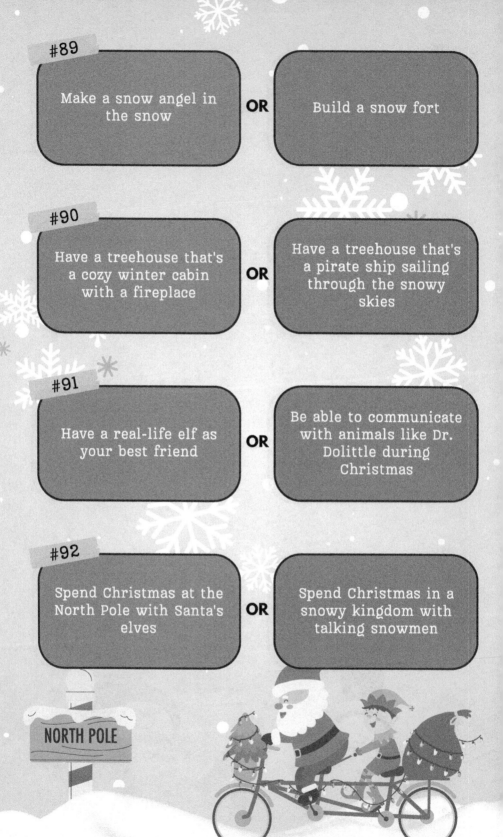

#93

Spend Christmas on a snowy mountain with singing snowflakes

OR

Spend Christmas in a candy cane forest with playful gingerbread people

#94

Be able to create your favorite holiday treats with a snap of your fingers

OR

Be able to instantly light up your Christmas tree in any color you choose

#95

Have a pet snowflake that can play music

OR

Have a pet candy cane that can turn into any flavor you want

#96

Have a giant candy cane as a stocking stuffer

OR

Have a big box of chocolates as a stocking stuffer

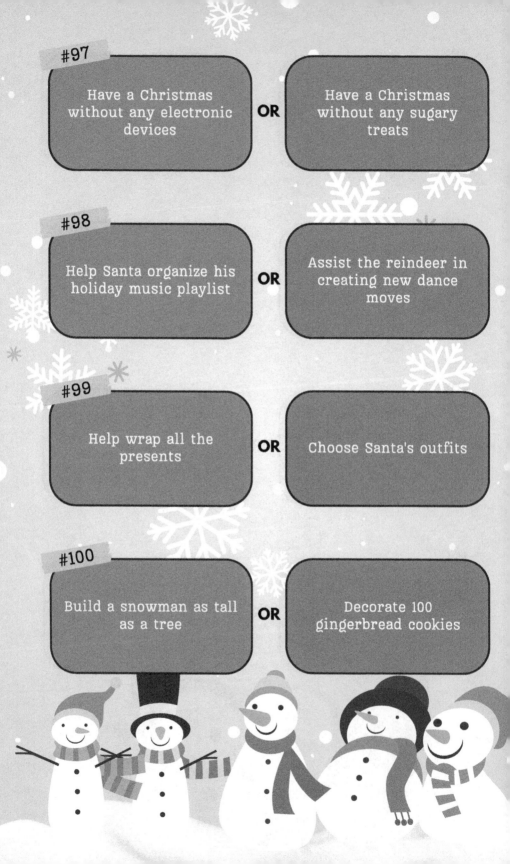

#97

Have a Christmas without any electronic devices

OR

Have a Christmas without any sugary treats

#98

Help Santa organize his holiday music playlist

OR

Assist the reindeer in creating new dance moves

#99

Help wrap all the presents

OR

Choose Santa's outfits

#100

Build a snowman as tall as a tree

OR

Decorate 100 gingerbread cookies

#101

Have a Christmas filled with magical surprises

OR

Have a Christmas with a superhero mission to save the day

#102

Spend Christmas in a cozy library with books that come to life

OR

Spend Christmas in a room with walls made of giant, talking gingerbread cookies

#103

Have a snowball fight with penguins

OR

Have a snowball fight with polar bears

#104

Have a snowy Christmas morning

OR

Have a sunny Christmas morning

NORTH POLE

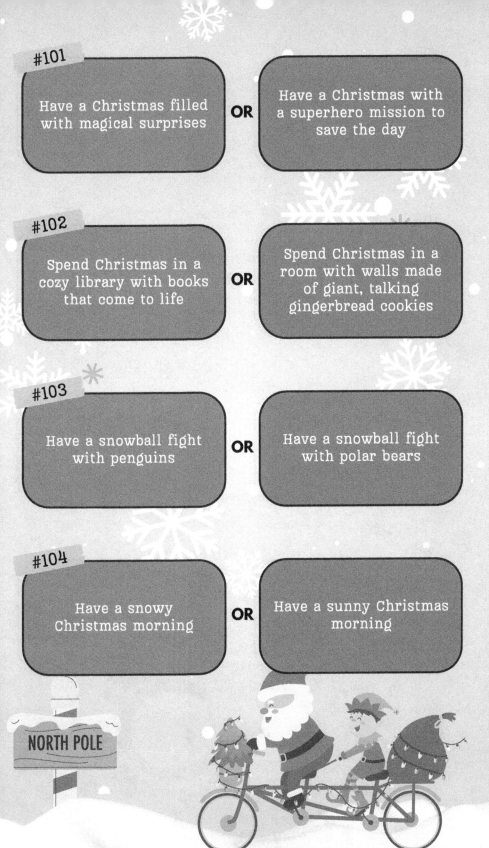

#105

Have a pet snowflake that can change color on command

OR

Have a snowman that can juggle snowballs

#106

Have a magical hat that can change your appearance

OR

Have a pair of glasses that reveal the true meaning of Christmas

#107

Have a big Christmas feast for breakfast

OR

Have a big Christmas feast for dinner

#108

Have a magical cape that can turn you invisible

OR

Have a holiday-themed wardrobe where you can instantly change your outfit

#109

Have a pet reindeer that can talk to you

OR

Have a snowflake that can make it snow on command

#110

Have a magic hat that can transform you into any holiday character you like

OR

Have a sled that can glide on rainbows

#111

Have a Santa Claus costume that transforms you into the real Santa

OR

Have a magical Christmas tree that grants your holiday wishes

#112

Help Rudolph find his missing nose

OR

Help Frosty the Snowman stay cool in the summer sun

#113

Have a Christmas tree that produces hot chocolate

OR

Have a Christmas tree that showers you with candy canes

#114

Be able to bring snow to a warm place on Christmas

OR

Be able to turn a cold place into a tropical paradise on Christmas

#115

Receive a present from your favorite fictional character

OR

Receive a present from your favorite real-life celebrity

#116

Have a treehouse with a cozy fireplace

OR

Have a treehouse with a built-in slide to the ground

NORTH POLE

#117

Have a holiday season that's always winter but never Christmas

OR

Have a season that's always Christmas but never winter

#118

Have a Christmas with a candy cane forest

OR

Have a Christmas with a chocolate river

#119

Have a snowstorm made of whipped cream

OR

Have a rain of candy canes on Christmas

#120

Have a treehouse in the shape of a giant candy cane

OR

Have a treehouse that's a giant gift box

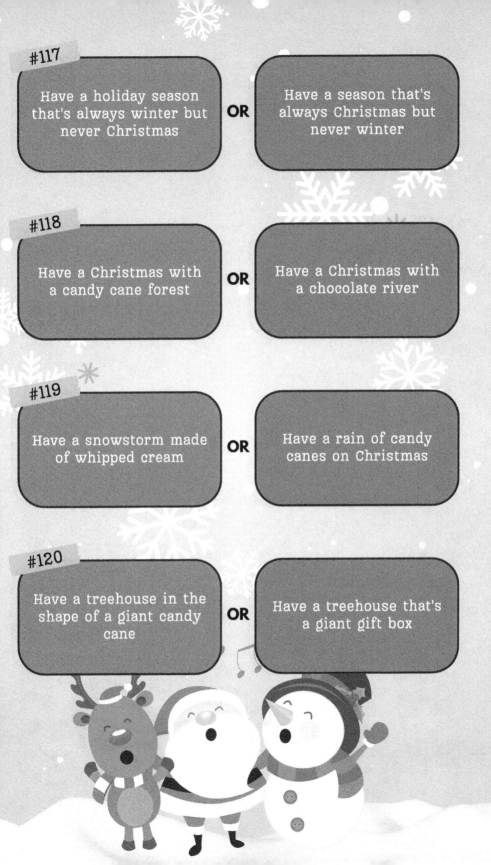

#121

Have a Christmas with talking toys that come to life at night

OR

Have a Christmas where animals can talk during the day

#122

Visit a village of musical snowflakes

OR

Visit a candy kingdom where the streets are made of chocolate

#123

Celebrate Christmas in a time when dinosaurs roamed the Earth

OR

Celebrate Christmas in a futuristic world with holiday robots

#124

Have a magic pen that brings your drawings to life as animated holiday stories

OR

Have a holiday cookbook that creates the tastiest treats you imagine

#125

Go on a magical sleigh ride with Santa

OR

Take a ride on a Christmas-themed train through a snowy forest

#126

Have a holiday-themed wardrobe where you can instantly change your outfit

OR

Have a magic box that can create any holiday decoration you want

#127

Have a Christmas tree that decorates itself

OR

Have a fireplace that tells holiday stories

#128

Have a pet snowflake that can perform beautiful snow dances

OR

Have a snowman that can sing your favorite carols

NORTH POLE

#129

Have a magical hat that makes your thoughts appear as written words

OR

Have a pair of boots that can take you to any place in your imagination

#130

Have a holiday season where it snows every day but never gets cold

OR

Have a season where it's always warm but snows marshmallows

#131

Have a snow day every day in December

OR

Have a day full of Christmas parties with your friends and family

#132

Receive a golden ticket to the North Pole

OR

Receive a key that unlocks a secret Christmas world in your backyard

#133

Have a Christmas with candy cane bridges and gumdrop pathways

OR

Have a Christmas with marshmallow clouds and chocolate rivers

#134

Be the conductor of the Polar Express

OR

Be the captain of a submarine exploring the depths of the ocean for hidden holiday treasures

#135

Have a snow globe that shows your dreams

OR

Have a cookie jar that always has your favorite treats

#136

Ride in a hot air balloon made of candy wrappers

OR

Ride in a boat that floats on a river of hot cocoa

#137

Have a magical ornament that can transform into any toy

OR

Have a holiday-themed wand that can create holiday surprises

#138

Spend Christmas in a fairytale castle

OR

Spend Christmas in a treehouse hidden in the enchanted forest

#139

Have a snowball fight with Santa's helpers

OR

Have a dance-off with the Gingerbread Man

#140

Be able to instantly decorate your home for Christmas with a wave of your hand

OR

Have the ability to make it snow on command

NORTH POLE

#141

Spend Christmas in a cozy library with magical books

OR

Spend Christmas in a holiday kitchen with animated cooking utensils

#142

Meet Santa Claus at the North Pole

OR

Receive a letter from him every day until Christmas

#143

Have a Christmas day where you can speak every language

OR

Have a day where you can understand animals

#144

Spend Christmas in a snow globe that's always snowy

OR

Spend Christmas in a snow globe that's full of flying reindeer

#145

Ride in Santa's sleigh

OR

Take a ride on a magical flying carpet during Christmas

#146

Have wrapping paper that sings when touched

OR

Have ribbon that sparkles like stars

#147

Have a magical snowflake necklace that grants you a special power

OR

Have a gingerbread house that can grow as tall as you wish

#148

Have candy canes for fingers

OR

Have snowflakes for toes

#149

Have a magical hat that can change your voice

OR

Have a pair of boots that allow you to jump to the top of the tallest Christmas tree

#150

Have a Christmas full of surprise guests

OR

Have a quiet Christmas just with your family

#151

Have a pet snowflake that can dance to your favorite tunes

OR

Have a snowman that can make delicious snow ice cream

#152

Have a Christmas tree that can grant you one special wish

OR

Have a fireplace that roasts marshmallows on command

NORTH POLE

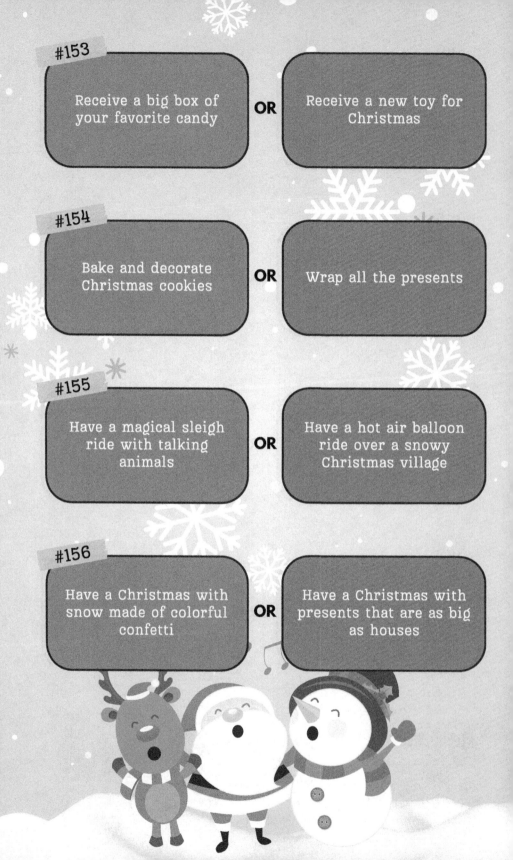

#153

Receive a big box of your favorite candy

OR

Receive a new toy for Christmas

#154

Bake and decorate Christmas cookies

OR

Wrap all the presents

#155

Have a magical sleigh ride with talking animals

OR

Have a hot air balloon ride over a snowy Christmas village

#156

Have a Christmas with snow made of colorful confetti

OR

Have a Christmas with presents that are as big as houses

#157

Go ice skating on a frozen lake

OR

Go sledding down a snowy hill

#158

Spend Christmas in a candy cane forest where everything is edible

OR

Spend Christmas in a holiday parade with talking holiday balloons

#159

Be able to talk to the stars on Christmas Eve

OR

Have a tree that blooms with presents

#160

Find a present as big as a house

OR

Find a thousand tiny presents

#161

Have a Christmas where everything is made of candy

OR

Have a Christmas where you can control the weather with a wave of your hand

#162

Have a magical ornament that brings your favorite toys to life

OR

Have a holiday hat that makes you instantly good at any game you play

#163

Find hidden presents in your house every day until Christmas

OR

Discover a hidden treasure map that leads to a surprise gift

#164

Have a Christmas with endless presents but no sweets

OR

Have a Christmas with lots of sweets but only one special gift

NORTH POLE

#165

Have a treehouse decorated with Christmas lights

OR

Have a gingerbread house with a candy cane fence

#166

Have a candy cane that never runs out

OR

Have a holiday sweater that always keeps you warm

#167

Have a snow day with talking snowflakes

OR

Have a day at the North Pole with the jolliest elves

#168

Have a Christmas with endless snow but no lights

OR

Have a Christmas with sparkling lights but no snow

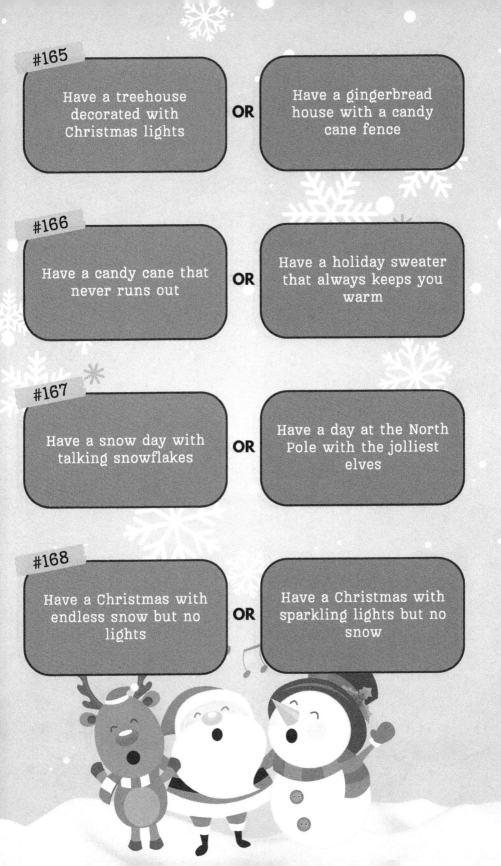

#169

Have a Christmas with sparkling lights but no decorations

OR

Have a Christmas with decorations but no lights

#170

Be an expert snow fort builder

OR

Be the world's best snow angel maker

#171

Be the lead in a Christmas play

OR

Be the director of the show

#172

Have hot chocolate that never cools down

OR

Have endless cookies

#173

Receive a special Christmas hug from Santa

OR

Receive a high-five from Rudolph the Red-Nosed Reindeer

#174

Have a Christmas tree that grows presents

OR

Have a fireplace that grants your holiday wishes

#175

Have a magical hat that makes you invisible

OR

Have a pair of boots that let you walk on clouds

#176

Spend Christmas Eve at the North Pole with Santa

OR

Spend Christmas in a cozy cabin in the snowy mountains with your family

NORTH POLE

#177

Have a magical sled that can take you anywhere in an instant

OR

Have a pair of magical boots that make you the fastest runner in the world

#178

Spend Christmas with characters from your favorite comic books

OR

Spend Christmas with characters from your favorite fairy tales

#179

Have Santa's magical powers for a day

OR

Be the CEO of a toy factory for a day

#180

Spend Christmas in a candy cane maze

OR

Spend Christmas in a gingerbread house with talking gingerbread people

#181

Spend Christmas with talking animals who can tell you stories

OR

Spend Christmas with fairies who can grant you one magical wish

#182

Be the star on top of the Christmas tree

OR

Be the lead reindeer guiding Santa's sleigh

#183

Help the Nutcracker guard the land of sweets

OR

Be a judge at a holiday baking contest

#184

Always wear a Santa hat

OR

Always wear reindeer antlers

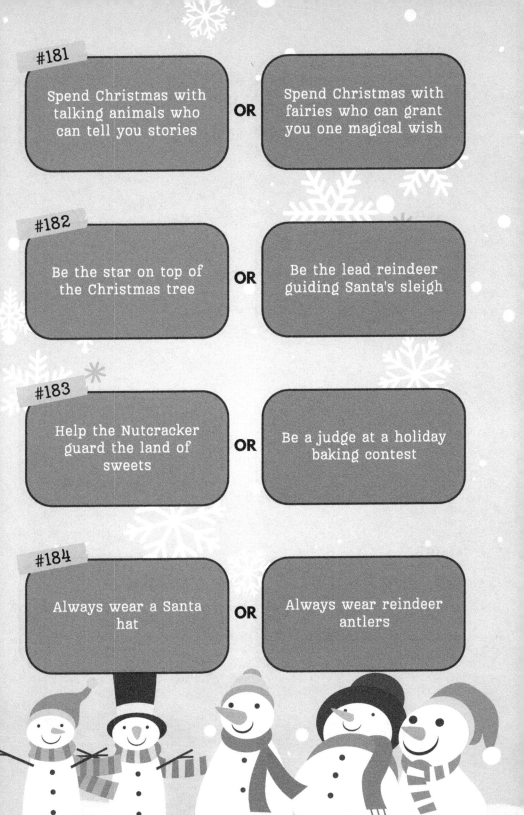

#185

Have a Christmas with unlimited hot cocoa but no snow

OR

Have a Christmas with endless snow but no hot cocoa

#186

Have a magical wreath that grants you three wishes

OR

Have a Christmas-themed teleportation device that takes you anywhere instantly

#187

Have a Christmas with a parade of toy soldiers

OR

Have a Christmas with a parade of marching penguins

#188

Have a sled that can slide on any surface

OR

Have a reindeer that can talk and tell you Christmas stories

NORTH POLE

#189

Have a Christmas with colorful candy snow

OR

Have a Christmas with glowing lights in the shape of your favorite holiday characters

#190

Be a character in "The Nutcracker"

OR

Be a character in "A Christmas Carol"

#191

Have a holiday season that lasts all year

OR

Have just one big day of celebration

#192

Have Christmas cookies that never crumble

OR

Have a Christmas storybook that never ends

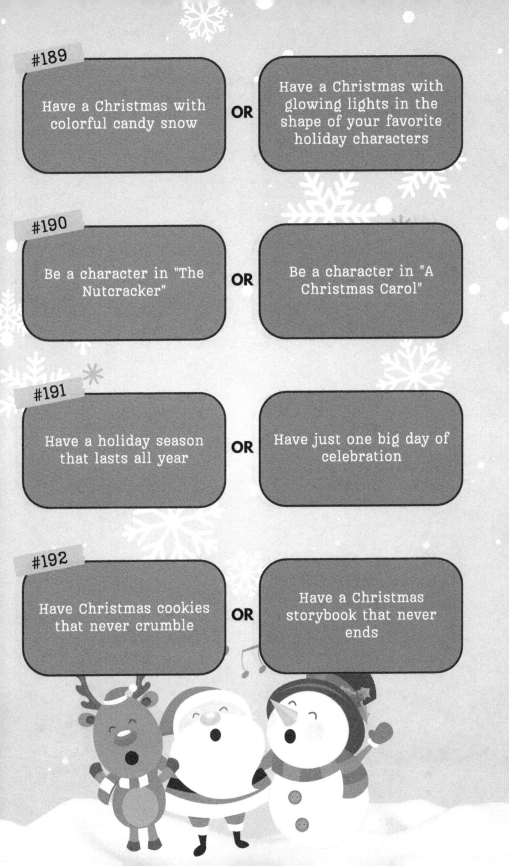

#193

Spend Christmas in a magical library full of books that come to life

OR

Spend Christmas in a room with walls made of giant, talking gingerbread cookies

#194

Have a sled that can fly through the stars

OR

Have a snowman that can create endless snowfall

#195

Have a reindeer that can fly you to school

OR

Have a snowman that can help you with your homework

#196

Meet Frosty the Snowman

OR

Meet Rudolph the Red-Nosed Reindeer

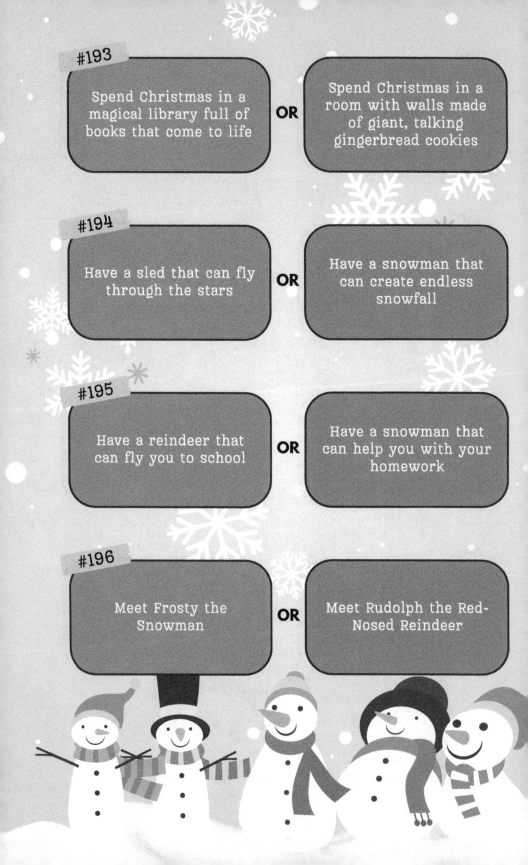

#197

Have a Christmas where you can speak to animals

OR

Have a Christmas where you can fly like a reindeer

#198

Have a pet reindeer for Christmas

OR

Have a magical talking snowman friend

#199

Have a treehouse that's a cozy winter cabin

OR

Have a treehouse that's a spaceship to explore the galaxy on Christmas day

#200

Have a Christmas where everyone wears pajamas all day

OR

Have a Christmas where everyone wears their fanciest outfits

NORTH POLE